They Came From DNA

Scientific American Mysteries of Science

They Came From DNA

by Billy Aronson

illustrated by Danny O'Leary

BOOKS FOR YOUNG READERS
Scientific American

W. H. Freeman and Company / New York

Dedication

To Lisa, who put the home in my chromosomes. (Before she came along, I was just a bunch of crosoms.) And to my whole family, who taught my *A*'s, *T*'s, *C*'s, and *G*'s their *P*'s and *Q*'s.
B. A.

For Mom, Dad, and Randi.
D. O'L.

Book design by Richard Oriolo

Library of Congress Cataloging-in-Publication Data

Aronson, Billy
  They came from DNA / by Billy Aronson.
     p.   cm.
  Includes bibliographical references and index.
  Summary: Explains genetics and how DNA works, through imaginary newspaper columns, letters from parent to child, and other scenarios.
  ISBN 0-7167-9006-8 (hardcover)
  ISBN 0-7167-6526-8 (paperback)
  1. Genetics–Juvenile literature. 2. DNA–Juvenile literature.
[1. Genetics. 2. DNA.] I. Title.
QII437.5.A77 1993
575.1–dc20   93-1038
                 CIP
                 AC

Printed in the United States of America

10 9 8 7 6 5 4 3 2 1

Contents

Introduction: My Mission

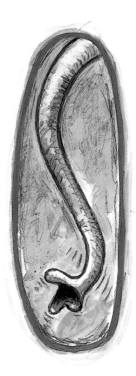

There I stood in the Intergalactic Yarkolizing Googletron, waiting to be yarkolized across the universe for the most important study of Earth creatures ever made. If all went as planned, I would discover Earth creatures' greatest secret.

In the remaining seconds before yarkolization a million thoughts raced through my mind.

I thought of the amazing photographs we'd already taken of Earth creatures by satellite.

I thought of the fascinating differences among Earth creatures. For example: A human's nose isn't nearly as long as an elephant's nose, while a frog's nose doesn't stick out from its face at all. Every other Earth creature feature—eyes, lips, arms, toes—showed this same striking variety.

I thought of the changes Earth creatures had gone through over our observation period: Ancient humans were shorter and had smaller chins than humans of today. Huge lizards called dinosaurs no longer existed. In fact, every kind of creature seemed to have changed.

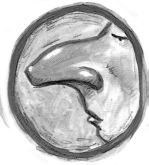

I thought of the questions I had been sent to answer . . . questions that had baffled our experts for millennia:

> What makes Earth creatures what they are?
> What makes Earth creatures so different from one another?
> What makes Earth creatures so different from what they were?

I looked forward to learning more about the Earth creatures with whom we were most concerned: humans. We had listened in on their simple languages and concluded that humans had developed what might loosely be called "intelligence."

I thought with sadness of the unfortunate researcher who had been sent to Earth before me, the late Bilch 3000. Bilch had been on the verge of a breakthrough when his mission ended in tragedy. In his final moments we received this transmission:

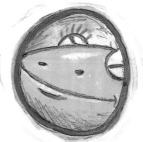

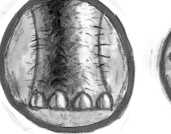

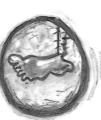

▼ Have found secret! All organisms on planet made of cells. Some made of only one cell.

▼ Most made of billions of cells.

▼ Every cell in complex organisms, such as dogs and humans, contains nucleus.

▼ Every nucleus contains chromosomes.

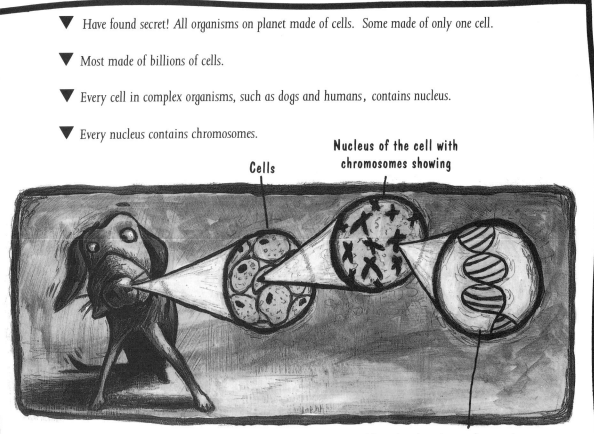

Cells

Nucleus of the cell with chromosomes showing

DNA molecules that make up chromosomes

▼ Every chromosome made of incredible chemical: DNA. DNA holds instructions for what creature is. DNA holds instructions for what creature will become. DNA holds instructions for what each creature looks like. How can chemical exert such control? By—

There his transmission abruptly ended with this chilling final image:

I shuddered as I thought about this picture. If humans see you, they can faint and squash you. To escape Bilch's fate, I knew I must avoid humans.

I was being yarkolized to a collection of abandoned writings called a Town Dump. Since it seemed humans rarely came near these writings, I would be able to scan for clues to what makes Earth creatures what they are—without risk of being found, fainted on, and squashed.

Town Dump

School Library

I clung tightly to a piece of paper I hoped I'd never have to use: a map of my study area. This map could direct me to a dangerous but exciting location—a School Library—which contained sets of writings packed with highly organized information, called encyclopedias. I'd been informed that the humans who inhabit the Library tend to be small, but warned that they too might faint and squash. I resolved not to risk a trip to the encyclopedias unless it became absolutely necessary.

Adding to the pressure was the incredibly short time I was being given to do my research: exactly 5.5 Earth days. Not one minute more or less. To avoid detection, I was bringing no communications devices. I would simply return to the exact spot where I'd landed and be yarkolized back home— exactly one hour before Kreeglestide.

Suddenly lights flashed. Sparks flew. Yarkolization had begun. As my body was zapped across the universe I felt nervous about my mission but optimistic: I would discover the secret of life on Earth and get home in time to wear my difriggled rebargitator in the Kreeglestide parade.

Or so I hoped. . . .

Part 1:

How Does DNA Get into Earth Creatures' Cells?

Day 1

Within seconds yarkolization was complete. I found myself in the Town Dump, inches from a majestic mountain of writings.

At once I began scanning for clues about the similarities and differences between humans and about the mysterious chemical, DNA, that Bilch believed controls them.

By midmorning I had uncovered my first piece of evidence:

Mom   Dad

HOME WITH SHERONA!

• • •

Sure, you've heard her super albums and seen her fabulous flicks. But you'll never know the real Sherona till you pay a visit to the one place where she can really be herself — at home with her family.

• • •

TZ: What's the greatest thing you've received from your parents?

SHERONA: My hair. I got my hair from my parents, and it's been a big help in my career right from the start.

TZ: But I mean, I've heard your father gave you a guitar when you were three and said you could do anything you put your mind to—

SHERONA: I got my dad's chin, and I'll always be grateful for that. Not that I hate my mom's chin or anything. I just wouldn't want it on the bottom of my face. Thank goodness I got my mom's nose, though, huh? Imagine me with Dad's nose! Ick!

TZ: But I mean, did your parents give you support?

SHERONA: If you mean like strong arches on my feet, yeah, definitely.

TZ: I mean love and understanding.

SHERONA: That too!

TZ: What about your brothers and sisters? You're a world-famous star. They're normal kids. Is there anything at all that you still have in common?

SHERONA: I share a lot with my brothers and sisters, and that's real important to me. For one thing, we all have Mom's great complexion. Except my sister Bobbi, whose face is totally covered with zits.

At first I found this article puzzling. How could Sherona get her hair from her parents? Do her parents grow extra hair, rip it off their heads, and glue it to Sherona's head? Do her parents grow extra chins, noses, feet . . . ?

But then I recalled Bilch's words. If this chemical, DNA, contains instructions about what a human looks like, then parents wouldn't have to give children their own actual hair. They could simply give their children their DNA.

I was also struck by the differences among the children in Sherona's family. There were differences in hair color, nose shape, chin shape. All but one had clear faces. That one face was covered with cute little red spots.

If these children had different looks, they must also have had different instructions for looks.

So each child's DNA must be different!

Another startling observation: Each child looked like one parent in certain ways and the other parent in other ways. Each must have gotten some DNA from one parent and some from the other.

But how?

How could two parents' DNA go together to make new DNA?

How could new DNA get from parents to children?

It occurred to me that if I was unable to obtain the answers to these questions, it was going to be a very depressing Kreeglestide.

I scanned furiously until late afternoon, when I uncovered a large piece of evidence containing that crucial three-letter word: DNA.

—Lickety-split!

L o w   P r i c e s ! *

1–10 copies	10 cents
11–50 copies	8 cents
51–200 copies	5 cents

*Unbound manuscripts, two days' notice, one side only, closed on weekends, staples extra, tax not included.

Could DNA be copied? I wondered. Do parents make extra for children? And if so, how?

Are there tiny structures that work like copying machines inside cells?

Darkness fell. I would have to wait till morning to continue my search.

As I leaned back on the heap, I began to consider the first words I should utter upon my triumphant return. Toward dawn, I came up with the phrase "One small step for a Skreeg, one giant leap for Skreeg-kind." Hmmm.

Day 2

I scanned all morning but found no further clues about how DNA is copied. So I made a daring decision: to risk a trip to the Library. My risk paid off—the encyclopedia revealed the spectacular secret of how a chemical can copy itself.

DNA

Deoxyribonucleic acid (DNA) is the extraordinary chemical that controls the traits of all living things on Earth. It controls the color of a rose's petals, the size of a wolf's fangs, the length of a giraffe's neck, and the shape of your toes.

DNA makes up chromosomes, which are found in the nucleus of every cell. There is a single long DNA molecule in each chromosome. Although a DNA molecule is thousands of times thinner than a human hair, it holds ten times as much information as this entire set of encyclopedias.

When scientists realized that DNA contains instructions for how an organism is made, they were anxious to find out what DNA looks like and how it works. When they finally figured out the molecule's structure, they were thrilled. Its unique structure gave them clues about how DNA copies itself.

It all happens in the nucleus of the cell.

When it gets ready to copy, the DNA untwists and separa*

The DNA molecule looks like a twisted ladder. Each rung is made of two bases.

As you can see, DNA is shaped like a twisted ladder. The steps of the ladder are made from bases called thymine (T), adenine (A), cytosine (C), and guanine (G). A pair of bases goes together in a certain combination to make up each step: Base T always goes with A, A always goes with T, C always goes with G, and G always goes with C. These pairings play a big role in the process by which DNA copies itself.

A base attached to its stretch of backbone is called a nucleotide.

As copying begins, the DNA strands unwind and the base pairs split apart. At this point the molecule looks like a zipper that is unzipping. Next, free nucleotides containing T's, A's, C's, and G's join unpaired bases on the strand. Free A's join with T's, free T's join with A's, free G's join with C's, and free C's join with G's.

Because each of the unpaired molecules on the strand will pair only with a certain free base, DNA can make an exact copy of itself. Soon there are two identical DNA molecules where there used to be only one.

In this way DNA's instructions can be copied. A cell can split and pass on the instructions for how an organism is made. These instructions can be passed from one generation to the next. The organism's family can grow!

Once the DNA is copied, the cell can split in two, leaving each cell with a complete set of DNA.

So DNA doesn't need a copier, I marveled. It can copy itself! Clearly, I'd been wrong about Sherona's parents. According to this new information, creatures don't send their DNA to other creatures' cells. When DNA copies itself, the whole cell splits so there are two cells, each with a set of DNA.

First, there's a cell.

The DNA in the cell copies itself.

Then the cell splits . . .

into two cells.

But what do creatures do with the extra cells? I wondered. And how do they get their DNA to their children?

When I got back to the dump, I scanned for clues about how humans pass their DNA to their offspring. When I came upon this handwritten note, I knew that I had, as they say on Earth, hit the crackpot.

Dear Emma,

Reading your letter made me miss you very much. The boys and Mommy miss you very much too. We can't wait till you get home from camp.

In your letter you asked me why Mommy can't have a puppy instead of another baby. Well, I'll try to explain.

You see, a mother and a father have special cells in their bodies. These cells go together to make a baby. A mother has egg cells. A father has sperm cells. A mother's egg cell and a father's sperm cell go together to make a baby.

Dog mothers and dog fathers have egg cells and sperm cells too. But dog egg cells and dog sperm cells are different from human egg cells and human sperm cells. When dog egg cells and dog sperm cells go together, they always make dog babies.

It's the same with cats, rabbits, bears, mice, parrots, elephants, ants, frogs, squirrels, giraffes, chickens, llamas, lizards, and even Bengal tigers. Each kind of animal has its own particular egg cells and sperm cells. Egg cells of one kind of animal go together with sperm cells of the same kind of animal. And when they go together, the babies they make are the same kind of animal as the parents. Animals whose sperm and eggs can go together to make a baby are members of the same species. Humans are a species. Dogs are a different species.

So if you want a puppy, your mother and I can't make you one. But we can find you one at the animal shelter when you get home!

Love,
Dad

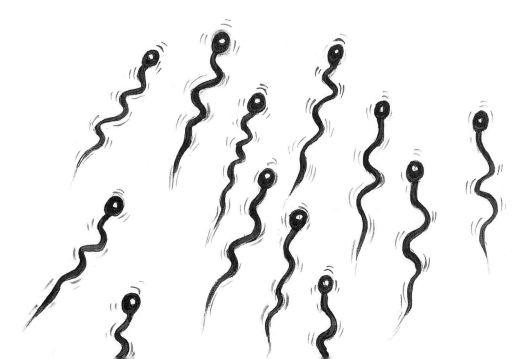

I don't know how much joy Dad's note gave Emma. But it sent *me* flomping across the Dump like a dromsiderp! I had learned about special cells called sperm cells and egg cells that carry instructions about what kind of creature (or species) the offspring will be!

I knew all cells contain DNA, so I reasoned that sperm cells and egg cells must contain DNA. When the sperm and egg come together, two sets of DNA from creatures of the same species unite. That's why off-spring are always the same species as their parents.

Also: Since a sperm comes from one parent and an egg comes from another parent, each can give some DNA, and the children can look like both parents.

Once again a new answer raised a new question: If two cells go together, does the new cell have twice as many chromosomes as other cells? Does it have twice as much DNA?

No, it doesn't. In this next writing I learned why it doesn't, and more. Much more.

ASK DOCTOR SUE!

Oh, Brother!

Dear Doctor Sue,

   I really want a sister, but all I have is brothers. When I heard my mom and dad were having a baby, I got excited. But it turned out to be just another boy!

   My friend Saundra says the father decides whether a baby is a boy or a girl. So I yelled at my dad. But he said it wasn't his fault! Who should I believe?

Signed,
Confused

Dear Confused,

   Don't take it out on your dad! Yes, in a way the father decides whether a baby is a boy or a girl. But it's not a decision he has any control over. Let me explain.

   Inside every cell in your body is a chemical called DNA, which holds the instructions that make you what you are. The DNA is twisted up into chromosomes.

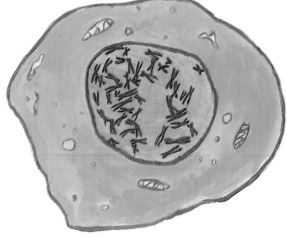

Both men and women have forty-six chromosomes in each cell. The only difference between men and women is the twenty-third pair.

In the cell, the chromosomes are every which way, but if you line them up by size, you can see the pairs.

Women and girls have chromosomes like these.

Men and boys have chromosomes like these.

The twenty-third pair of chromosomes in a man's cells consists of one chromosome shaped like an *X* and one shaped like a *Y*; the twenty-third pair in a woman's cells consists of chromosomes that are both shaped like *X*'s.

Male has

The only human cells that don't have twenty-three pairs of chromosomes are sex cells: the egg cell in a woman and the sperm cell in a man. They have twenty-three unpaired chromosomes—half the number of chromosomes other cells have. The twenty-third chromosome in an egg cell will always be an *X*, but the twenty-third chromosome in a sperm cell can be an *X* or a *Y*.

Female has

To start a baby, a man's sperm cell and a woman's egg cell join to make a new cell—with twenty-three pairs of chromosomes, forty-six chromosomes in all. That new cell copies itself over and over to make a baby. If the twenty-third pair of chromosomes is two X's, the baby will be a girl. If it includes one X and one Y, the baby will be a boy.

A sperm cell with a Y chromosome from your father met your mother's egg cell. That joining of sperm and egg started your brother. If a sperm with an X had met your mother's egg, your brother would have been a sister.

Since the twenty-third chromosome contributed by a man can be either an X or a Y but the twenty-third chromosome contributed by a woman can only be an X, it's the man's contribution that determines whether the new cell will grow to be a boy or a girl.

Your father's sperm contributed that first Y chromosome that determined the sex of your new brother. But your father couldn't control this if he wanted to! Better apologize for screaming at him.

Yours in sickness and health,

Doctor Sue

had found the key: The sex cells Sherona's parents used to make her contained half the number of chromosomes of a regular cell. So when the two sex cells got together, the new cell had twenty-three pairs of chromosomes—like all the other human cells.

This writing also revealed another precious fact: Earth creatures start out as a single cell. Sherona's parents didn't need to get their DNA into each of Sherona's cells. They used one sperm and one egg to make a single cell. Then that cell copied itself over and over to make Sherona.

But suddenly a problem entered my mind. It bothered me. Then it baffled me. Then it shook my very padoodles. (And I am one whose padoodles are rarely given to shaking.)

The problem was this: I knew that each cell of each human being has one set of instructions from each parent—that's two complete sets of instructions. But each human has only one chin, one nose, one hair color. Why do they need an extra set of instructions? I wondered. How do they know which set of instructions to follow?

As I scanned the odd-shaped heaps in the Dump with ferocious determination, in search of a clue that would answer these questions, I found myself unconsciously chanting the slogan I had not chanted since my days at Scanning School: I think I scan. I think I scan. I think I scan. . . .

oward sunset I came upon three writings. They did not answer my burning question but did serve to confirm my understanding of Earth creature reproduction. Well, the first two did. . . .

THE CARSON COUNTY COURIER

Elmer Alston's Horses, Bingo and Bessie, Announce Birth of Brownie

Both Bingo and Bessie were thrilled.

ThE DAILY TIMES SENTINEL

King and Queen Announce Birth of Prince

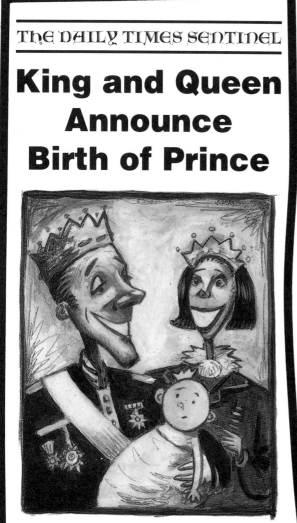

Both King and Queen were thrilled.

his writing made perfect sense to me. As I would have predicted, the human father's DNA and human mother's DNA joined to make DNA that controlled the formation of a new human.

his writing also confirmed my information. A father horse's DNA and a mother horse's DNA joined to make DNA that controlled the formation of a new horse.

THE NATIONAL CONSPIRER

Hollywood Star and Starlet Announce Birth of Rhinoceros Child

Both star and starlet were concerned.

This writing caused me great distress. A human father's DNA and a human mother's DNA join to make human DNA. According to the letter to Emma from her dad, DNA from a man and a woman could not control the formation of a baby rhinoceros.

This rhinoceros-child story contradicted all previous evidence. Sherona's parents had only human children. The confused girl who wrote to Doctor Sue had only humans in her family. The horses on Elmer Alston's farm formed other horses.

Did a piece of preposterous writing like this really belong in a Town Dump?

I concluded that this writing must be different from the others. It must have been written simply to cause humans to laugh.

I suppose that the idea of two humans having a rhinoceros baby *is* funny. As I consider it now, I myself could almost be taken by a mild fit of chuckling.

Through the night I lay back in the mud, stared up at the stars, and reviewed my progress over the first two days. I had solved a major part of the puzzle. I had figured out how Earth creatures pass on their looks.

Bilch had been correct: Cells in every Earth creature contain DNA.

DNA is passed from parents to children, and copies of DNA are made for every cell in Earth creatures' bodies. The key is DNA's structure. The DNA molecule is shaped like a twisted ladder. It unzips and copies itself like this:

The DNA molecule . . . .

unzips . . . .

and copies.

Because DNA copies itself, new cells can be created and creatures can live and grow.

DNA is passed from parents to children.

Sherona's mom

Sherona's dad

The egg comes from the mother.

The sperm comes from the father.

Sherona has DNA from her mother and her father.

Sherona

Since the new creature's DNA is made of DNA from each parent, the creature looks in some ways like each parent.

Each species of creature has its own particular type of egg cells and sperm cells. So creatures mate with their own species to produce offspring that are of the same species as their parents.

In humans, DNA is divided up into twenty-three pairs of chromosomes. Both of a female's twenty-third pair of chromosomes are shaped like X's. One of a male's twenty-third pair is shaped like an X and one is shaped like a Y.

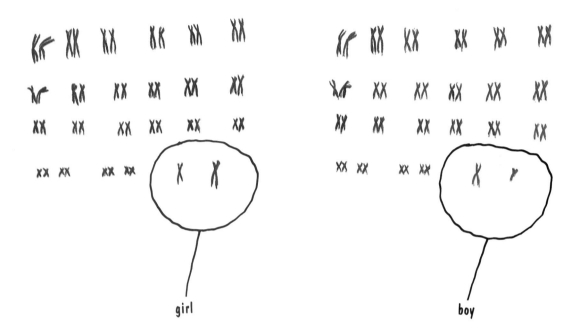

girl

boy

If a new child gets the Y, it will be a boy. If it gets the X, it will be a girl.

But huge questions still loomed:
I had no idea how DNA controls looks.
I had no idea how children decide which parent to look like.
I had no idea how DNA changes Earth creatures over time.
I had no idea why writings in the Town Dump had such a disgusting odor. *Phew!*

Part 2:

How Does DNA Control
What People Are?

At the crack of dawn I began the next major step. I knew DNA controls the way Earth creatures look. But I had to find out how. How could a tiny molecule control the shape of a nose or a chin?

My scanning led me to a new word that would be linked to DNA at every step in my historic quest.

Wish you had curly hair?
Sure. Who doesn't!

Tired of curlers and sprays and gels? Sure. Who isn't!

Ever paid a fortune for a perm that turned your hair into a ball of knotty frizz? Sure. Who hasn't!

If you answered yes to any of these questions—and who didn't!—you just might be ready for an exciting new operation that can curl your hair *so it stays curled.*

You just might be ready for a permanent that's really permanent. You just might be ready to sign up for a "hair-raising" visit to the incredible folks at

GENE-O-CURL!

When you walk into the GENE-O-CURL clinic, our highly skilled geneticists will take a quick look at your genes. They'll know just which gene is responsible for that hopelessly straight hair of yours. Then they'll get right to work changing that surly gene into a curly gene! Within weeks your hair will be curly for keeps!

Plus, if you're among our first hundred customers, the GENE-O-CURL geneticists will be glad to throw in a permanent change of hair color at no extra charge!

So send your deposit of $2,000 now! Get your name on the waiting list for a GENE-O-CURL curl—so your DNA will be A-OK!*

*Actual operation may not be available until well into the next century, if ever.

So it seemed that these "genes" control whether hair is curly or straight. But *DNA* controls traits! Do genes control DNA? I wondered. Does DNA control genes? Do genes control chromosomes? What are genes, anyway?

And how, I thought, do genes (or DNA) control hair curliness, straightness, and color? Is hair made of genes? Is hair made of DNA?

This case of a clown showed that DNA has even more power over Earth creatures than I had suspected.

Clown Quarterly

Vol. XXI, No. 22

He can't juggle. He can't jump. But he sure can scrunch his lips in different directions. Maybe that's why the clown that Clown Quarterly readers ask about more than any other is that legendary lip-meister himself, Scrunch the Clown.

Up Close with Scrunch

CQ: When did you realize you had the ability to scrunch your lips apart in different directions?

SC: I used to scrunch my lips in different directions in the cradle—I could drool out of both scrunches simultaneously. In nursery school I used to impress the other kids by sipping milk through the bottom scrunch while sucking my thumb through the top scrunch.

CQ: But surely that super-scrunch of yours took years of hard work to learn, didn't it?

SC: No. You can learn to blow up balloons. You can learn to drop your pants. You can learn to take a cream pie in the face. You can even learn to fall down a flight of stairs while carrying a layer cake. But lip scrunching is one of those abilities you've just got to be born with---like the ability to raise one eyebrow or curl your tongue. It runs in my family.

CQ: Ha, ha!

SC: I'm serious.

CQ: Sorry.

SC: Dad was in vaudeville. He couldn't tell a joke to save his life. But he could scrunch his lips like it was going out of style. My grandma was a great scruncher too. She could kiss you good night and get lipstick on both of your earlobes.

CQ: She sounds like quite a woman.

SC: She loved to tell us about her uncle Max in the old country who conducted the Royal Orchestra without using a baton—only his lips.

I had already learned that looks, such as hair color and chin size, can run in a family—and be controlled by DNA. But this writing seemed to be saying that an ability, the power to "scrunch" lips, can run in a family.

Incredible—a molecule that could control physical abilities and skills!

The previous writing surprised me. This one sent a shring through my darples.

Identical twins who have been separated at birth
are reunited at the punch bowl.

I found this picture absolutely astonishing. I stared for hours, but was unable to find a single difference between the twins. "Identical twins" must really be identical, I concluded. They must have the exact same DNA.

The twins had been apart since the day they were born. So they couldn't have spoken to each other about what to wear to the party. Yet they still came up with the same idea!

If this was possible, DNA had power over more than looks. It had power over more than abilities. It had power over humans' thinking.

Could DNA really control the workings of the mind? If so, how?

That afternoon a fluffy gray blob floated over the Dump and began spitting. I found this blob spit refreshing until my blats began to wrinkle (I hate wrinkly blats). So I grabbed a box from the heap and held it over myself as I continued to scan.

Eventually I chanced to look up at the box—and discovered information about the amazing stuff from which all Earth creatures are made!

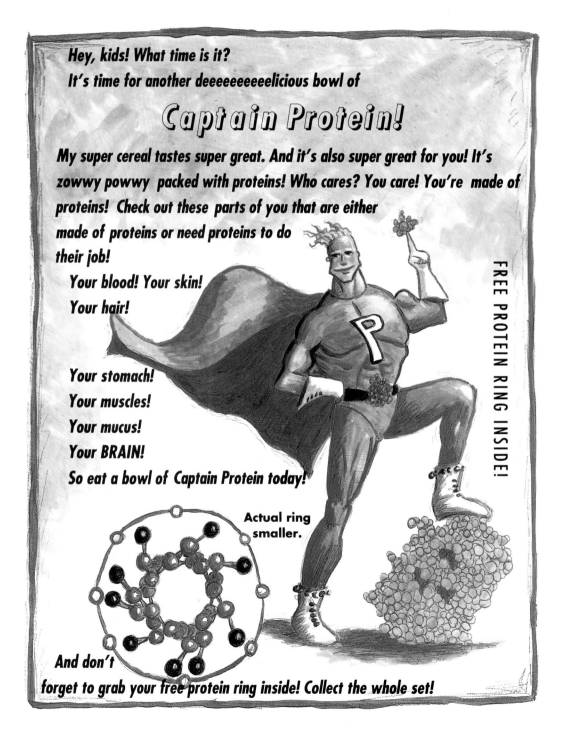

Hey, kids! What time is it?

It's time for another deeeeeeeeelicious bowl of

Captain Protein!

My super cereal tastes super great. And it's also super great for you! It's zowwy powwy packed with proteins! Who cares? You care! You're made of proteins! Check out these parts of you that are either made of proteins or need proteins to do their job!

Your blood! Your skin!
Your hair!

Your stomach!
Your muscles!
Your mucus!
Your BRAIN!
So eat a bowl of Captain Protein today!

Actual ring smaller.

FREE PROTEIN RING INSIDE!

And don't forget to grab your free protein ring inside! Collect the whole set!

An unexpected breakthrough!

I'd found that human hair, whether curly or straight, is made of proteins.

The human brain, which controls ideas, is made of proteins. Human muscle, which controls the ability to scrunch lips, is made of proteins. Humans must be made of proteins, I concluded. And if DNA controls the making of humans, I figured, it must somehow control the making of proteins.

That night the cloud's spitting tapered down until it was more of a warm drool. I crawled into the box to keep my blats dry till dawn.

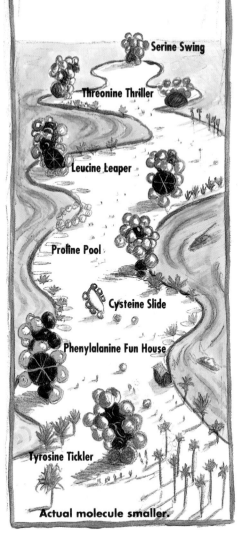

Hey, kids, it's still not too late to enter the Captain's Contest! First powwy protein prize is a free week in my fabulous fun park, Proteinland! Proteinland is the world's only fun park that's shaped like a protein molecule—with an amazing amusement on every amino acid!

Serine Swing

Threonine Thriller

Leucine Leaper

Proline Pool

Cysteine Slide

Phenylalanine Fun House

Tyrosine Tickler

Actual molecule smaller.

Day 4

At sunrise I wriggled out of the soggy box and got back to my scanning. Soon I came upon a writing that made me marvel at the precision of protein producers.

OUTLAWS OF A DIFFERENT STRIPE

MAPES IS LED AWAY, BLUSHING. IT'S ALL OVER.

SPOT IS LED AWAY, BLUSHING. IT'S BLACK AND WHITE AND RED ALL OVER.

Police arrested Millhouse Mapes today for last Tuesday's robbery of the First Finest Bank. Although Mapes insists he was in Miami caring for his "poor sick granny" at the time of the robbery, police have matched his fingerprints to fingerprints found in the bank men's room. Witnesses testified that before making his getaway, the masked bandit stopped to go to the bathroom. Mapes's fingerprints are identical to those found on the First Finest flusher.

Also arrested was Spot, the zebra that is believed to have assisted Mapes in making his getaway. Although the zebra was also

(cont. p. B12)

(**Outlaws** from p. B2)

masked, the bank camera recorded a close-up of its stripes. Zebra stripes are as unique and distinctive as human fingerprints—no two zebras have the same pattern. When the stripes in the video were found to be identical to Spot's, the arrest was made.

Should the charges stick, both Mapes and Spot will be wearing stripes.

Unique prints on humans, unique stripes on zebras . . . I could hardly believe the precision with which the proteins that make up Earth creatures' skin are arranged. How could DNA make proteins with such precision?

Unable to find a shred of evidence that addressed this question in the entire Dump, I resolved to risk another trip to the Library.

The encyclopedias were a protein prober's paradise.

PROTEINS

Proteins are the basic building-block molecules that make up all living things. Your body needs a steady intake of proteins to keep growing and working properly. That is why it is important to eat such high-protein foods as beans, milk, eggs, and meat.

Though there are many different proteins in your body, all are made of combinations of twenty different small chemicals called amino acids.

The construction of proteins in your body is controlled by a large molecule called DNA. In the precise arrangement of the bases that line its strands—*T* (thymine), *A* (adenine), *C* (cytosine), and *G* (guanine)—DNA contains coded instructions for making all the proteins in your body.

DNA molecules are found in the nucleus of a cell, but proteins are made outside the nucleus in an area called the cytoplasm. The long DNA molecule is far too large to slip through the small holes, called pores, in the wall of the nucleus. So DNA passes its message about how a particular protein is to be constructed to a molecule that serves as a messenger. Messenger ribonucleic acid (mRNA) is similar to DNA in structure but thinner—with a single strand instead of two strands—and much shorter.

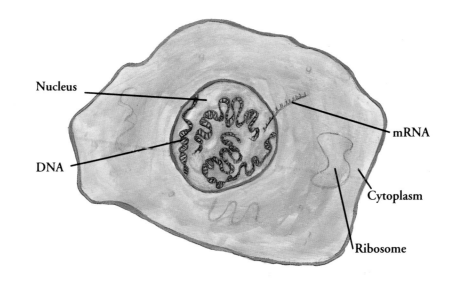

Nucleus

mRNA

DNA

Cytoplasm

Ribosome

Messenger RNA doesn't need to be nearly as long as DNA because a single strand of mRNA is not a copy of all the instructions for all the proteins that make up the body. It is a copy of only one set of instructions for one protein—the protein needed by a particular cell.

③ The mRNA detaches from the DNA.

④ The mRNA moves out of the nucleus while the DNA zips up.

① A part of the DNA strand unzips.

② Free nucleotides attach to the open DNA then link together to make mRNA.

Here is how DNA passes its instructions for making a certain protein to mRNA. First the DNA molecule unzips a small part of itself. Then free nucleotides come in and attach. Nucleotides with G's attach to C's, C's attach to G's, uracils (U's) attach to A's, and A's attach to T's, all along the unzipped part of the DNA. The only difference between the bases on DNA's nucleotides and those on mRNA's is that mRNA includes the base uracil instead of the base thymine. The mRNA detaches from the DNA. Finally, the DNA zips again, and the mRNA moves out of the nucleus.

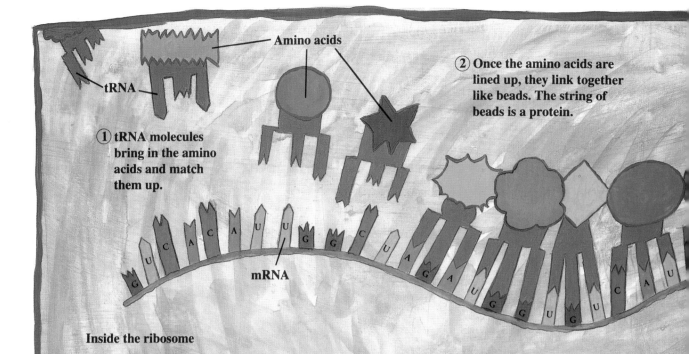

Amino acids

tRNA

② Once the amino acids are lined up, they link together like beads. The string of beads is a protein.

① tRNA molecules bring in the amino acids and match them up.

mRNA

Inside the ribosome

The mRNA carries its message through a pore in the nucleus's wall and into the cytoplasm, to a structure called a ribosome.

The ribosome is the cell's protein factory, where the mRNA's instructions are read and the protein is constructed. Each set of three bases along the mRNA strand makes up the code for a particular amino acid. As each set is read, a molecule called transfer ribonucleic acid (tRNA) brings whichever amino acid is called for to the ribosome.

Then the next three bases on the mRNA strand are read, and another amino acid is brought in.

The ribosome attaches the amino acids together one at a time, as though they were links in a chain. When the ribosome is finished reading and attaching, the chain is complete. A protein has been formed.

The different proteins constructed by this process make up all different parts of you, from the hair on your head to the skin on the bottom of your feet.

The segment of a DNA molecule that has instructions about a certain trait is called a gene. Somehow the DNA in each cell knows which gene to unzip. Scientists don't know how the DNA knows, but they're working on it. In the meantime, you should be thankful that the DNA does know which part of its strand to use. Otherwise you really might have a foot in your mouth!

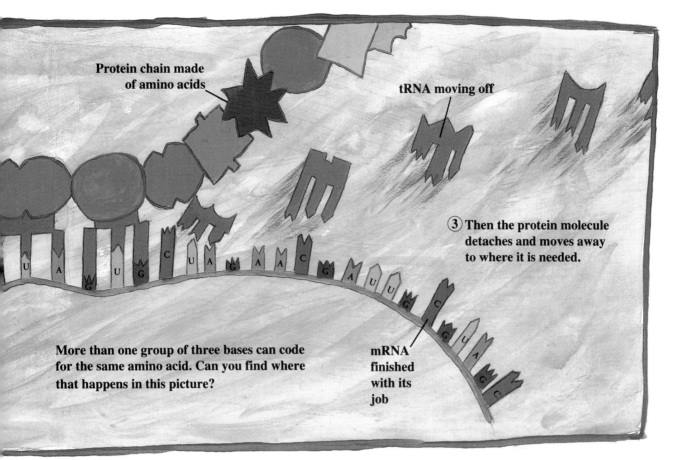

Protein chain made of amino acids

tRNA moving off

③ Then the protein molecule detaches and moves away to where it is needed.

More than one group of three bases can code for the same amino acid. Can you find where that happens in this picture?

mRNA finished with its job

As they say on Earth, YOU REAKER!! So proteins are building blocks of Earth creatures. Amino acids are building blocks of proteins.

A gene is a section of DNA and part of a chromosome. A gene controls curly hair.

The process by which DNA makes proteins is incredibly precise. Amino acids, which make up the large protein molecules, fit together like pieces of a puzzle. DNA controls which pieces go where by sending their message to the ribosomes on mRNA. That's how specific proteins are made with such precision. That's how DNA controls Earth creatures' makeup.

But that nagging question continued to nag: What determines whether a creature will have its mother's version of a trait or its father's? Each cell's DNA ladder contains genes from each parent for every trait.

How does mRNA know whether to carry the message from the mother's gene or from the father's gene—to make protein for the mother's or the father's version of the trait?

Nag, nag, nag. Some questions just won't stop nagging.

Finally, I came upon a writing that silenced the nagging. A clue to why a creature looks like its mother or its father!

TV Guidance, Oct. 15

Life is Ruff

Princess and Rover finally become parents in tonight's hour-long special episode of *One Stray at a Time*. But joy turns to tears as Rover is baffled by the appearance of brown puppies among the litter. Princess explains that black-furred parents can have brown-furred puppies because brown fur is recessive and black fur is dominant. A Labrador retriever will have black fur, the dominant color of fur for Labs, if it has two genes for black fur—or if it has one gene for black fur and one for brown. If a pair of black Labs that carry the gene for brown fur mate, they might each pass the recessive gene to their pups. Any pup with two genes for brown fur will have brown fur.

(Princess: Roseanne Bark, Rover: Luke Furry; WK9, 9 P.M.)

44

The key to the nagging mystery was this: Some genes are dominant (pushy). Others are recessive (quiet).

When both the dominant gene and the recessive gene are present, the dominant gene wins out.

So why can Princess and Rover both have the dominant fur color (black) and produce puppies that have recessive fur color (brown)? Princess and Rover must each have a recessive gene, I decided. Only puppies with two recessive genes—one from each parent—will show the recessive characteristic.

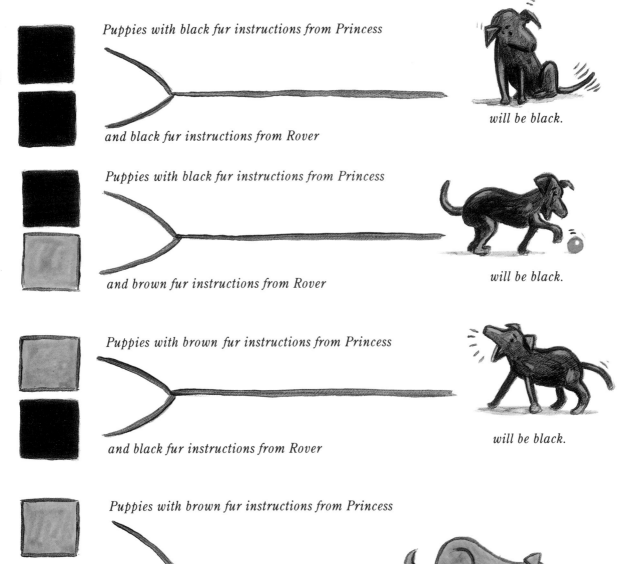

Puppies with black fur instructions from Princess

and black fur instructions from Rover

will be black.

Puppies with black fur instructions from Princess

and brown fur instructions from Rover

will be black.

Puppies with brown fur instructions from Princess

and black fur instructions from Rover

will be black.

Puppies with brown fur instructions from Princess

and brown fur instructions from Rover

will be brown.

Then, just when I thought I knew all there was to know about how genes control Earth creatures, I found this:

MAN RUNS LIGHT, BLAMES MOM!

Drivers often make excuses when stopped by the police. But when Officer Jinny Johnson pulled over nineteen-year-old Belcher McFadden this morning, she was shocked by his excuse.

"I stop the guy for running a red," recounts Johnson, "and he blames his mom! The woman who brought him into the world! What's our society coming to, b'jeepers?"

As ridiculous as McFadden's blaming his mother may sound, he's not backing down. In fact, he called a press conference today, at which medical celebrity Doctor Sue explained McFadden's logic. "Belcher has a special kind of color blindness that makes red and green look exactly the same. This condition is genetic—you're born with it. Women rarely have it, but they can carry it in their genes and pass it on to their sons. When boys have the gene from their mothers, they are always color blind. So in a way, Belcher's mother did cause his color blindness, but—"

At this point McFadden interrupt-

Officer Jinny Johnson scolds Belcher McFadden.

ed, ranting, "See? My mom's the reason I keep calling evergreen trees ever-reds! My mom's the reason I keep calling the American flag the green, white, and blue! And my mom's the reason I keep running red lights!"

Another CBRLR (color-blind red-light runner) who wished to remain anonymous expressed regret that he had not blamed his mother. "I admire Belcher's guts," he explained. "I'm red with envy."

This one had me stumped. Why would certain characteristics tend to show up only in members of one sex?

Could this have something to do with the chromosomes that determine a human's sex—that twenty-third pair? I wondered. The gene that causes someone to see red and green as the same color must be found on the X chromosome in that twenty-third pair of chromosomes. That way, a girl would be color blind only if her father was color blind and her mother carried the gene. A boy would be color blind if his mother carried the gene, whether or not his father was color blind.

One thing I was sure of was that Belcher McFadden should not have blamed his mother. Like the father who "caused" his daughter to have a brother, this man's mother had no control over which genes she was born with or passed on. McFadden was, as they say on Earth, passing the belch.

So I'd answered the second question: How does DNA control looks? Plus, I'd learned that it controls even more than looks!

I spent the night tracing the steps by which I'd pinned down my historic answer: I'd found that DNA is in the nucleus of cells of every Earth creature.

To make children, parents combine their DNA. A male and a female of the same species contribute a sperm cell and an egg cell, each containing a single set of chromosomes. The two sex cells go together to create a new cell, which has two sets of DNA. This cell copies itself over and over till a new organism is formed that has DNA—and characteristics—from both parents.

But before the new cell can copy itself, the DNA inside it must copy itself. Its strands split apart, allowing free nucleotides containing bases to pair with bases on each strand, till two new DNAs result—which are identical to the first.

and copies.

splits . . .

DNA . . .

This DNA determines a creature's traits by controlling the production of proteins that make up the creature. Proteins are basic building blocks from which all Earth creatures are made. In humans, hair is made of proteins. So is skin. So are muscles. That means that curliness of hair, shape of fingerprint, and ability to scrunch lips depend on proteins. It's the same with all other traits in humans and other Earth creatures.

Different sections of DNA called genes contain instructions for making specific proteins that determine specific traits. DNA's message is carried from inside a cell's nucleus to outside by a similar, smaller molecule: mRNA.

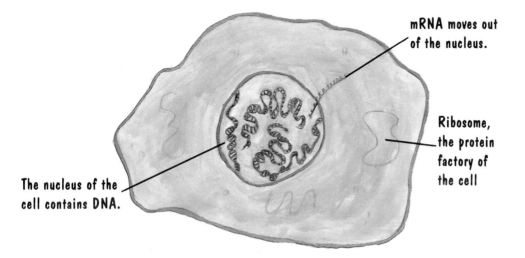

mRNA moves out of the nucleus.

Ribosome, the protein factory of the cell

The nucleus of the cell contains DNA.

The mRNA carries the DNA's message to a ribosome, where proteins are made, and tells the ribosome how to line up amino acids in a particular order to form a protein.

tRNA brings amino acids and lines them up according to the instructions on the mRNA. The amino acids link together, and the protein is complete.

Some genes dominate others. This causes some colors, sizes, shapes, or abilities to appear more commonly in a species. For Labrador retriever fur, it works like this:

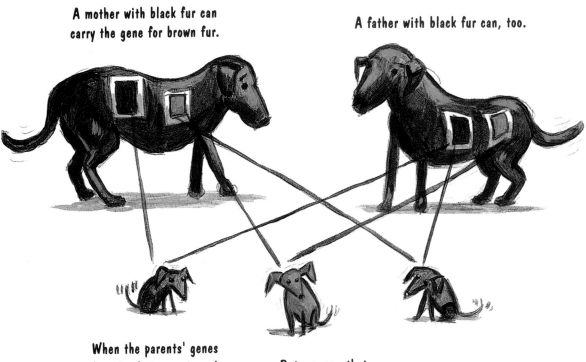

A mother with black fur can carry the gene for brown fur.

A father with black fur can, too.

When the parents' genes combine in their puppies, those who have even one black-fur gene will have black fur.

But a puppy that gets both brown-fur genes will have brown fur.

Some characteristics tend to appear in creatures of only one sex. The instructions for these characteristics must appear on the twenty-third chromosome with the instructions that determine sex.

But there were still unanswered questions:
I still didn't know if there were more reasons that Earth creatures are the way they are.
I still didn't know how DNA had changed Earth creatures from what they were long ago.
I still didn't know why the small humans who inhabit the Library hailed me with the strange greeting, "Halloween was last week."

Part 3:

How Does DNA Change a Species Over Time?

Day 5

So far the Town Dump had been good to me. Its clues had helped me to figure out how Earth creatures pass on their DNA and how DNA controls their traits. But still I wondered: Would the Dump yield clues about how Earth creatures changed over time?

Once again, the Dump delivered.

It looks like any hospital. But it's not any hospital. It's a hospital somewhere in *A WORLD BEYOND*.

Woman: I'm so nervous about our baby. That radiation I was exposed to while I was pregnant—

Man: There's no point in getting yourself all worked up, honey.

Nurse: Mr. and Mrs. Smith! I've got some rather disturbing news about your baby.

Man: Tell us, please.

Woman: Is our baby all right?

Nurse: You asked for it.
Man: Oh no, this is awful!
Woman: It's hideous!

Man: When he's driving, he won't be able to gaze at the scenery while he's watching the road ahead!
Woman: When he's dancing, he won't be able to look at his feet while he's staring into his sweetheart's eyes!

Man and Woman: Our son is a mutant!

Nurse: He can always get work in a circus. . . .

THE END . . .
or the beginning!

What was this "mutant"? I wondered. The key was clearly the absence of a third eye. The lack of a third eye in this species seemed to be an undesirable, rare trait.

Does it appear only in those of a certain sex, like color blindness? Is it recessive, like brown fur on Labrador retrievers?

No. Color blindness and brown fur are not caused by radiation. Those traits do not cause such alarm and shock.

I concluded that a mutant must be a creature with an entirely new and unexpected characteristic.

The next piece of evidence I found was tiny and gooey. But it provided facts that stuck in my mind even more tightly than the gunk in the paper stuck to my darples.

Mutant Karate Frog Bubble Gum

Of course you know about the Mutant Karate Frogs' mutations.

Radiation gave them traits that are very weird for frogs: human height, human weight, and the ability to do karate.

But you probably didn't know that you've got mutations too! Most mutations aren't caused by radiation.

They're just tiny goofs in the way the chemical DNA that's inside you copies itself. Usually they don't make any visible difference in your body at all!

If you liked that fact, you'll love Mutant Karate Frogs 4—The Curse of the Flying Phlegm! Catch it this summer!

So mutations can be harmful, harmless, or helpful, I had discovered. Mutations don't always have an external cause; they may be simple mistakes in the DNA.

That afternoon I came upon three writings that contained crucial clues. The mystery of how DNA changes a species was unraveling right before my blats.

ROACH TERMINATOR

Hasta La Vista, Buggy!

Note: Product may lose efficiency if used continuously over a two-year period. The few cockroaches that are immune to the poison can survive, reproduce, and generate an entire immune strain of cockroaches.

TO USE ROACH TERMINATOR:
Separate Roach Terminator packets and distribute in kitchen, bathroom, and anywhere else roaches may appear.
At once roaches will be lured to poison bait. Within hours you'll be saying "Hasta la vista!" to your roach problems.
Replace packets every three months.

Put Roach Terminator in your

Kitchen   **Bathroom**   **Basement**

The note on the box gave me a clue to how a species could change. Cockroaches could become immune to a poison. But is immunity to poison a mutation? I wondered. Or is it caused by a recessive gene?

Either way, this evidence suggested to me that a mutation could help an Earth creature survive a dangerous change in the environment. Creatures with the changed gene would survive, mate, and produce more creatures like themselves. Soon what was a small change in a small number of creatures would become common in the species.

No one knows for sure why the dinosaurs died out. Maybe they died because the earth changed in some way, and the dinosaurs couldn't change quickly enough to adjust.

Whatever the cause, now all that's left of the largest creatures who ever walked the earth is a few of their bones.

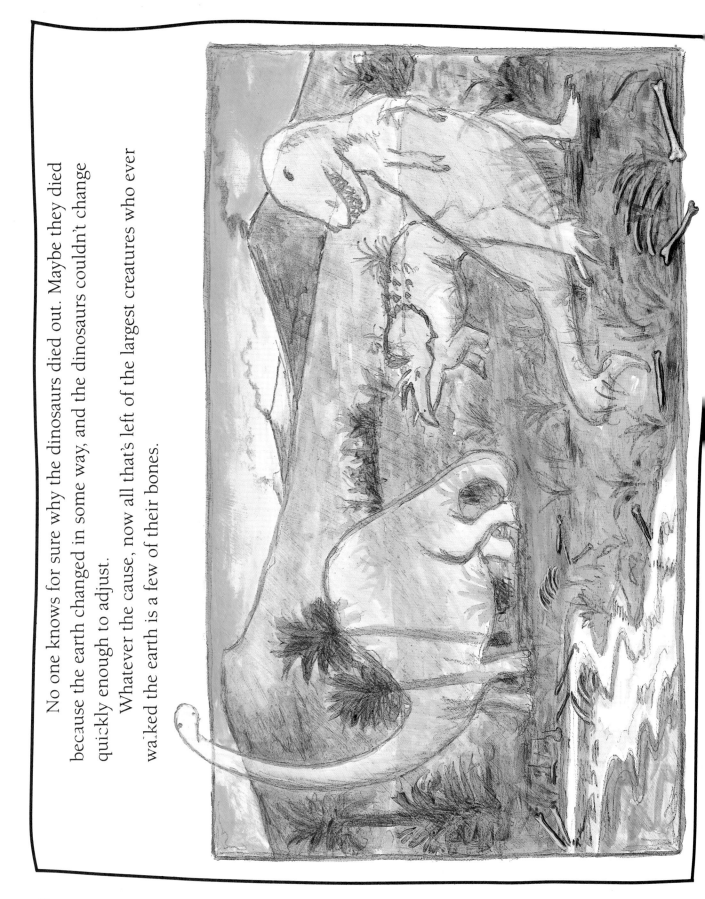

At first glance it seemed that this writing about dinosaurs and the writing about cockroaches had nothing in common. This one was about huge creatures who lived long ago. The other was about tiny creatures who live today.

Yet suddenly it struck me that they had something important in common. I wasn't sure why it struck me, but it struck me. And it kept on striking me. "Stop striking me!" I wanted to shout. (An idea that won't stop striking you can be worse than a question that won't stop nagging.)

But just then I realized why this idea that the dinosaurs and the cockroaches had something in common kept striking me: Because they did! Both the cockroaches and the dinosaurs lived in changing environments.

The package of roach poison said that if certain changes happen to the genes of cockroaches, they can survive a deadly change in their environment. If those changes don't happen, the cockroaches can't survive the change.

The writing about the dinosaurs said that perhaps dinosaurs did not survive a change in their environment. Is that because their genes did not change in a way that would have helped them live in their changed environment?

I decided that the greater the variety of characteristics a species has, the more likely it is that *some* members of the species will be able to survive a change in the environment.

The greater the variety in a species, the less likely it is to die out completely, as the dinosaurs did.

Therefore, variety—caused by mixing of mothers' and fathers' DNA and by mutations—is *good* for a species, because variety makes it more likely that a species will survive.

I was puzzled by the form of the next writing. It seems that after being ordered to read a short text, subjects are compelled to answer questions about what they have read. Perhaps it is a form of torture.

GSE

General Smartness Examination

Section 1: Reading Comprehension
Time: 1 hour
Read each passage carefully, then circle the best answer for each question. If you are having difficulty with any individual passage, skip it and proceed to the next. When you are finished with this section, close your book.

DO NOT PROCEED TO THE NEXT SECTION.

Do you like corn? Of course you like corn. Everyone likes corn. Even the people who make up these tests like corn. There's nothing like the pleasure of chomping into the juicy kernels that line a long cob of corn.

But did you know that the first cobs of corn weren't that long at all? In fact, scientists have found five-thousand-year-old corncobs that are less than one inch long!

What changed corn? People did.

Native Americans first began growing corn about seven thousand years ago in what is now New Mexico. Soon they noticed many differences between different cobs of corn. They noticed that different cobs had different-colored kernels. They noticed that different cobs had different numbers of kernels. And they noticed that different cobs were of different lengths.

The Native Americans made great use of the differences they observed. In particular, they made use of the differences in length. They found that when they used only longer cobs as parents, the offspring corn tended to be longer. If they were careful to use only the longest cobs as parents generation after generation, the corn got longer and longer. They were changing the species of corn itself!

Now, centuries later, the average cob of corn is ten times longer than its ancient ancestor. Thanks to centuries of this process, you can butter and salt a long cob of corn!

1. The best title for this passage would be
    (a) How People Changed Corn
    (b) How Corn Changed by Itself
    (c) How Corn Changed People
    (d) A Kernel of Truth

2. The relation between ancient Native Americans and corn is the same as the relation between
    (a) Livestock breeders and cattle
    (b) Rain and frogs
    (c) Detectives and criminals
    (d) Teachers and ringworm

3. Which of the following is probably true?
    (a) Corn could be made smaller using the same process
    (b) Corn could be made yellower using the same process
    (c) Corn could be made sweeter using the same process
    (d) All of the above

Clearly the best title (although not a very interesting one) was "How People Changed Corn." The writing was about how humans take advantage of different traits to change species.

It made me think of the way roach poison changes species, by allowing only roaches with a certain trait to survive.

But how did humans change over time? Did someone carefully select mates so human species would change like corn? Did their environment change, killing most humans and allowing others with certain traits to survive, so human species would change like cockroach species?

Only one day remained before I was to be yarkolized back home. I was closing in on my answer. But Kreeglestide was closing in on me!

Day 6

The next morning I stumbled upon a wondrous word on a small, rhyme-infested slab of facts.

EVOLUTION

Music: Mick Frebbles
Lyrics: Skuz K

You say you want an evolution?
Well, you know,
Species are changin' all the time.
It really changed our constitution;
Well, you know,
It brought us up out of the slime!
As all different cavemen would fight for the food supply,
The strong ones would win, don't you know that the
weak would die.
Then the winners were feelin' great,
'Cause of all of the food they ate,
And you know they would start to mate!
(Guitar solo)

DNA

Music: Mick Frebbles
Lyrics: Zitz

D-N-A . . .
All my troubles seemed so far away . . .

So finally I had a name for the process that changes creatures: evolution. As people with different traits fought for food, the strongest won and reproduced.

Humans were changed in the same way cockroaches change, not in the way corn changed. Environment—in this case food supply—made the difference.

A mere four and a half hours remained before Kreeglestide.

I realized that if I were absent from the Dump, I would not be yarkolized back.

I realized that if I were not yarkolized back, I would be stuck with the stink of the Dump for this Kreeglestide—and perhaps for several zillion Kreeglestides to come.

But I was a Skreeg possessed. I had to make certain that this "evolution" could explain Earth creatures' change over time.

I had to risk a final trip to the Library. I had to take the step that would seal my fate. . . .

The encyclopedia provided confirmation—and more. Much more. Much, much, much, much more. More.

Evolution

Evolution is the theory that a species changes over time, usually as a result of the species' ability to adapt to the environment. According to this theory, individuals that are best suited to their environment survive, while those less suited die out. The survivors mate and pass on the traits that allow them to survive to their offspring. After several generations all members of a species may have the desirable traits; less desirable traits may disappear from the species completely.

What does the theory of evolution have to say about you? It says that the various ancient primates whose bones have been found are your ancestors. Some of these primates had special abilities, like the ability to walk upright or to use tools. Those who had these abilities were better able to survive than those who lacked them. Over thousands of years, as primates with these advantages survived and mated, they became more and more adept and intelligent. When they became extremely adept and intelligent, they were human beings!

This trip to the Library confirmed that the species best suited to their environment survive.

It confirmed that a species can be changed by the environment as cockroaches are changed by poison. It confirmed that a species can be changed by the environment as corn was changed by Native Americans. It confirmed that a species that is unable to change dies out as the dinosaurs did.

It also confirmed that some humans faint when sighting creatures from another planet. Others hop up and down while emitting piercing shrieks and yanking hairs from their heads.

Grateful for their enthusiasm but wary of being fainted on, I retreated to the Dump.

It was a mere 2.3 hours before TUMMY (Totally Unchangeable Moment of Major Yarkolization) when I found a stirring suggestion on the back of a small box:

MAPPING THE MYSTERIES WITHIN

Journey with your host to the mysterious world within your cells! Team up with scientists on an exciting mission to map human chromosomes! Why map our chromosomes? Because knowledge of the locations of certain genes along the DNA strand could be used to prevent disabilities, cure diseases, or even create life.

". . . And now, having mapped every corner of the frail blue ball upon which we tread, adrift in an ever-expanding ocean of space, we turn our focus inward and embark on the even more awesome venture of mapping the genetic material that wields ultimate power over the very essence of what we are, what we may be, what we have been, and what we might have become—but at what cost?"

RUNNING TIME: 60 MINUTES

So Earth scientists were trying to map chromosomes to find the locations of individual genes. It reminded me of the Gene-O-Curl writing. People could curl hair permanently if they knew which gene was responsible for the trait.

If they knew the locations of every single gene, they might be able to figure out how genes work and begin to control traits. Maybe they could create an entire human with whatever appearance and abilities they wanted.

If they could control genes, they could control life!

Next I came upon a small card that had interesting information—and a sweet smell.

PLAYERS OF THE FUTURE!
Toppers' Fantasy Extra!

NAME: Buddy Baker   **POSITION:** Center Field
BATS: Left, Right   **THROWS:** Left, Right

Year	Club	At Bats	Stolen Bases	Doubles
2218	Mets	502	199	64
2219	Mets	525	258	68
2220	Mets	540	324	101
2221	Mets	568	170	62
2222	Mets	602	444	111

Triples	Bases on Balls	Home Runs	Runs Batted In	Batting Average
12	101	104	308	.801
16	101	144	405	.904
48	204	288	466	.799
14	287	186	554	.848
77	312	333	674	.999

Buddy Baker has broken every major-league single-season batting record and threatens to break every lifetime record as well. Buddy is proud that his phenomenal batting, fielding, running, and attitude have led the New York Mets out of the cellar. His one regret is that the team has been unable to finish better than sixth.

n his spare time Buddy plays banjo, bakes pies, and collects ocks shaped like the heads of American presidents. He comes from Orlando, Florida, where his genes were manipulated.

This card suggested something else that might someday really occur—should humans learn the locations of their genes. If the genes that control certain skills could be located and understood, skills could perhaps be improved.

In the remaining hour I scanned for further writings about uses humans might someday make of genes—and stumbled upon an ingenious use they're *already* making . . . .

Congress of the United States
House of Representatives
Washington, DC 20515-3210

Congresswoman Vanessa Venora

Dear Committee for Kindness to Creatures,

I have read your letter. If I understand correctly, you are opposed to a common scientific practice: the splicing of genes in bacteria cells in such a way that the bacteria are made to produce insulin. You feel this practice is cruel to the bacteria and would like me to propose a law banning it.

I must tell you that were I to propose such a law, my words would quickly be drowned out by laughter. Here's why.

1. Insulin is badly needed to fight diabetes, a disabling, life-threatening disease. The method to which you object is a cheap and effective method of producing this valuable chemical.

2. Before scientists discovered this method, they had to take insulin from dead pigs. Surely that method would be even more vigorously opposed.

3. Bacteria are just single-celled organisms! Their bodies are made of one little cell! Bacteria have no brain cells! They have no nerve cells! They have no heart cells! They are unable to experience the feelings you attribute to them, such as "pain, humiliation, and total loss of self-respect." They are unable to "toil by the sweat of their brows." They have no sweat! They have no brows!

I hope this explanation satisfies you and that you will call off the protests you have been holding outside my office, my husband's office, and my daughter's nursery school.

Sincerely,

Vanessa Venora

Clever humans! They were more intelligent than I had thought. They'd found a way to use genes to cause cells to produce proteins the cells don't usually produce.

Humans manipulate other creatures' genes to get those creatures to produce certain protein substances that humans can use as medicine.

I dreamed that our scientists might someday be able to manipulate human genes to get humans to produce electrostatic fur, which we could use as padoodle muffs.

With mere minutes remaining, I began again to imagine the speech I would make upon landing—a speech that would be broadcast live across my entire planet, throughout the rest of the galaxy, and perhaps even in neighboring galaxies on pay-per-view:

Skreegs, Bilches, Garfinkles, lend me your floms!

I have found out how Earth creatures pass on their traits!

DNA is a ladder-shaped molecule in every cell of every Earth creature that controls the creature's makeup.

Earth creatures get their DNA from their parents.

Cell

DNA

Nucleus

Cytoplasm

Ribosome

The DNA strands separate.

Free nucleotides come in

and attach to the single strands,

making two new DNA molecules just like the first.

Before DNA can be passed from a creature to its offspring, a DNA molecule must make an identical copy of itself by splitting.

I have found out how DNA controls what Earth creatures are!

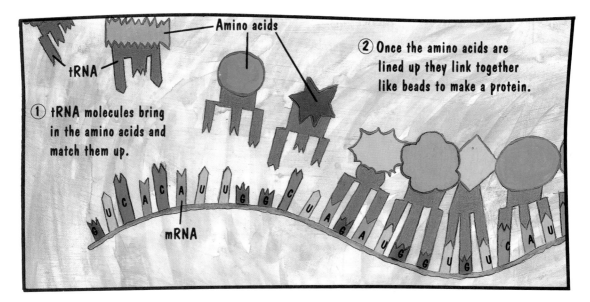

It does this by controlling the construction of the basic building-block molecules from which all Earth creatures are made: proteins. An individual segment of a DNA molecule that controls the makeup of a particular protein is called a gene.

To make a protein, DNA in the nucleus of a cell passes the code for the protein to a much smaller molecule: mRNA. The mRNA carries the message to a ribosome, where protein construction takes place.

By passing information about the proteins that make up various parts of organisms—from the brain to fingerprints to muscles—DNA determines Earth creatures' looks and abilities.

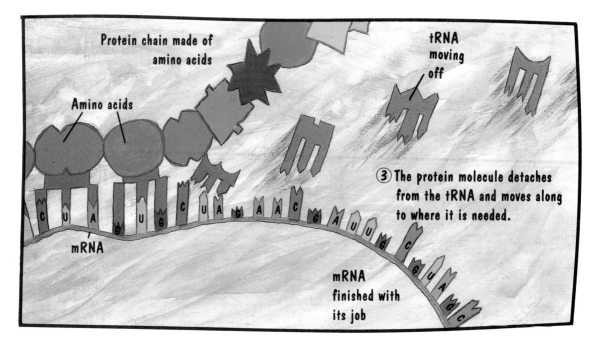

And I have learned how DNA changes a species!

When DNA is changed—by radiation or accident—a new version of a trait may appear. This new version is called a mutation.

Some mutations are harmful, some are harmless, some are helpful.

Mutations add to the variety in a species. Creatures with certain versions of traits are able to survive better in an environment than others. These creatures reproduce as others die out, until the entire species has the useful version of the trait.

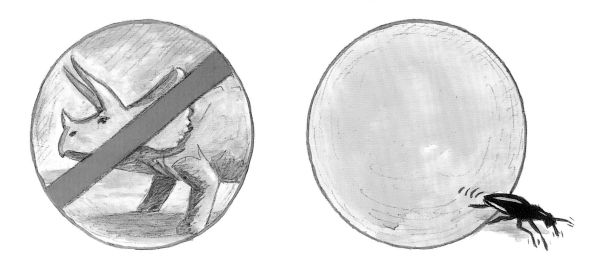

Over time some species cannot survive changes in their environment—they die out. Other species change and become better suited to the environment. This process is called evolution.

Humans know how to change a species by choosing certain members of the species to be parents. They also know how to make other species' genes work to their own advantage. They are discovering which genes affect which of their own traits—and could use this information for the good of their species.

My glorious thoughts were interrupted by a deafening roar—and the sight of a hideous, massive creature crawling toward me across the slime. I dove deep into the heaps of writings but could hear the beast inching closer and closer. . . .

I peered out to discover that the "creature" was an Earth vehicle that had come to donate more writings to the Dump. As it departed, I climbed out and scraped writings from my body. A card I plucked from my left blat gave me cause for alarm:

Seasons Greetings From Our Family to Yours!

I panicked. Clearly, the children did not share many of their parents' physical traits. Yet they did seem to share certain unique abilities.

Do humans sometimes come together to form a family because they share certain abilities? Do humans gain certain abilities from those around them?

This raised a question I hardly dared consider with mere minutes before yarkolization.

Could parents affect offsprings' abilities in some way other than through DNA? Could individuals other than parents affect a creature?

Could simply living in their environment and learning from it help make creatures what they are?

But the confusion caused by this writing was overwhelmed by the horror caused by the next. . . .

Part 4:

How Can DNA Transform a Space Creature?

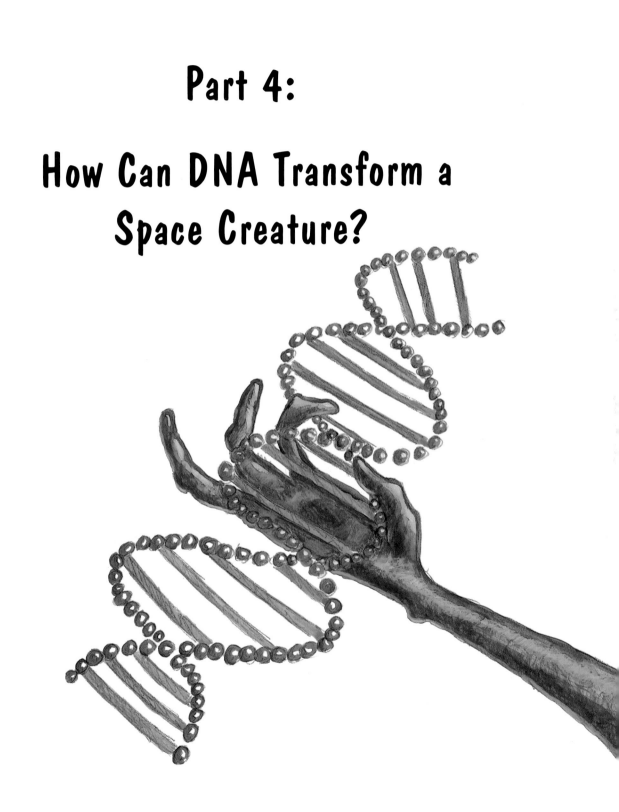

It was then that I beheld atop the newly deposited heap of writings the photograph of a figure I knew well . . . because it was my own.

Daily Times Sentinel

EXTRATERRESTRIAL SEEN IN ELEMENTARY SCHOOL LIBRARY

Several students and teachers in the library of the Carson County Elementary School witnessed the appearance of a space creature today. Police officer Jinny Johnson arrived on the scene after the departure of the alien but traced the creature's footprints back to the Town Dump. Johnson then organized an emergency squad consisting of recently paroled prisoners Millhouse Mapes and Spot the Zebra; medical celebrity Doctor Sue; infamous color-blind mother-blamer Belcher McFadden; visiting performers Scrunch the Clown, Cellz 2 Men, Roseanne Bark, Luke Furry, and Sherona; and a girl who simply

wishes to be known as No Longer Confused About Why I Have So Many Brothers. The squad is surrounding the dump and about to close in.

My blats shook. My darples froze. My padoodles drooped to the ground. On the horizon, closing in all around me, was the strangest assortment of creatures ever assembled on any planet in the universe.

The following article is typical of those you've been noticing in magazines and newspapers lately.

Come with TeenZeen as we go . . . MEETING SKREEG!

Sure, you've seen Skreeg on all the major talk shows and seen his sensational story in documentaries and TV dramas and blockbuster movies and Broadway musicals. But you won't know the real Skreeg till you join *TeenZeen* on a trip to Beverly Hills—and the cool, comfy castle known as Spaceland.

TZ: What's your favorite thing about people?

SKREEG: Their DNA. The way it makes exact copies of itself so that traits can be passed from one generation to the next. The way it determines those traits by controlling the creation of the proteins. The way it has changed the species by providing mutations and other variations that allow the species to survive changes in the environment and even be made stronger by them.

TZ: But I mean, you've chosen to desert your native planet to stay here with people. Isn't there anything about people that you really enjoy?

SKREEG: I enjoy collaborating with humans on various undertakings.

TZ: Research? Teaching? Mapping out our DNA?

SKREEG: Surfing, sunning, dancing till we drop.

Dear Fan,

I hope you've enjoyed this record of my discoveries.

Though I sometimes miss my difriggled rebargitator, with you infinitely varied Earth

creatures every day is more exciting than a Kreeglestide parade! Best wishes to

you and your incredible DNA.

Love,

Skreeg

Glossary

amino acids. The small molecules that fit together to make up proteins.

bacteria. One-celled creatures too small to be seen without a microscope. Scientists have figured out a way to put a human gene into bacteria DNA. Then the bacteria can make proteins humans need.

base. A small molecule that makes up part of the large molecule DNA and the smaller RNA molecules. The order of bases on the DNA and RNA strands carry the instructions that make you what you are. Bases include adenine, thymine, guanine, cytosine, and uracil.

base pair. Two bases that fit together to make a rung of the DNA ladder and that are joined together when DNA copies itself. Adenine goes with thymine, and guanine goes with cytosine.

blat. Any body part containing one or more darples.

chromosome. A tube-shaped structure made of DNA that is found in the nucleus of the cell. There are 46 chromosomes in a human cell.

cytoplasm. The area of a cell that is outside the nucleus.

darple. That which protrudes from a blat but is completely unconnected to a padoodle.

DNA. Deoxyribonucleic acid, a molecule shaped like a twisted ladder that encodes information about heredity. It is the code in the DNA (together with the environment you grow up in) that makes you what you are.

dominant gene. The pushy gene. Everyone has two copies of each gene. If the two copies are different, the cell uses the dominant copy.

dromsiderp. A large vibrating derp.

gene. A length of DNA that codes for a characteristic, such as hair color.

gene mapping. The process of figuring out the order of genes in a chromosome.

geneticist. Someone who studies heredity and variation in animal and plant species.

immunity. Resistance to a disease.

molecule. The smallest amount of a substance that is still that substance, but is bigger than an atom. Molecules are made of atoms. Large molecules such as DNA are made of small molecules.

multicellular. Made of many cells.

mutation. Any change to the order of bases on a DNA strand.

nucleotide. The unit of the DNA molecule. The nucleotide is made up of a base and the sugar and phosphate backbone to which it is attached.

nucleus. The central portion of a cell that contains the DNA.

organism. An individual that can perform all life functions by itself.

padoodle. A doodle tipped with a single pa. Though a doodle tipped with a double pa is often called a padoodle, it should actually be referred to as a "papadoodle." Though a pair of papadoodles that share pas is often referred to as a "papadoodle pair," it should actually be referred to as a "papadoodlepadoodle" or simply a "papadoubledoodle."

protein. A big molecule made up of linked amino acids.

recessive gene. The quiet gene. Everyone has two copies of each gene. A recessive gene will only be expressed if both copies are of the recessive type.

sex chromosomes. The chromosomes that decide whether an individual is male or female. Two X chromosomes make a female, and an XY combination makes a male.

species. A group of individuals whose egg and sperm cells can meet to make new individuals.

trait. A distinguishing characteristic, such as hair color or chin shape.

Index

Page numbers in italics refer to illustrations.

For Further Reading

The best advice that Skreeg and all of his friends at Scientific American Books for Young Readers can give you is to read further. It is a good way to find out more about the world around you.

These three books for young readers can give you a straightforward account of genetics and heredity:

Asimov, Isaac. *How Did We Find Out About Genes?* New York: Walker Books, 1983.

Backwill, Fran. *DNA Is Here to Stay.* Minneapolis, Minnesota: CarolRhoda, 1993.

Bornstein, Sandy. *What Makes You What You Are: A First Look at Genetics.* New York: Julian Messner, 1989

This book was written by one of the people who discovered that DNA was shaped like a twisted up ladder called a double helix. It's meant for adults, but you can enjoy it too. It shows how scientists go about figuring things out:

Watson, James. *The Double Helix.* New York: Atheneum, 1968.

It is impossible to find out everything about DNA from books. There are lots of scientists studying DNA right now, and new discoveries are being made all the time. The best way to find up-to-date information is to use the *Readers' Guide to Periodical Literature,* which you can find in your school or public library. It will tell you where to find recent magazine articles on DNA. The major newspapers, such as *The New York Times* and the *Wall Street Journal,* also have indexes that you can find in the library. Your librarian can help you use these reference books.

And keep your eyes open. Skreeg learned a lot by reading whatever he could find that had anything to do with his topic. You can do the same.

A Note to Readers, Teachers, and Parents

As you may have figured out by now, Skreeg is made up. As far as anyone knows (and there are lots of scientists looking very hard), no alien has ever landed on Earth. In fact, though many scientists think that there may be intelligent life out there, they haven't found it yet.

And the documents that Skreeg finds are made up, too. They may be a lot like articles and letters and cereal boxes that you have read, but they are all made up.

But we are not writing this note to tell you about the made-up part of *They Came From DNA*. We are writing this note to assure you that what Skreeg discovers is not made up. Everything in the book about DNA is true, at least as far as scientists have been able to figure out so far. We were so concerned about our science being accurate that before we printed this book, we sent it to a geneticist so that he could read it and look at the pictures and make sure that we hadn't made any mistakes.

The scientist who checked *They Came From DNA* for accuracy is Dr. Art Champlin, and he is the Leslie B. Arey Professor of Biological Sciences at Colby College in Maine. We are grateful to him for keeping the science in this book true.

The Author, the Artist, and the Editors